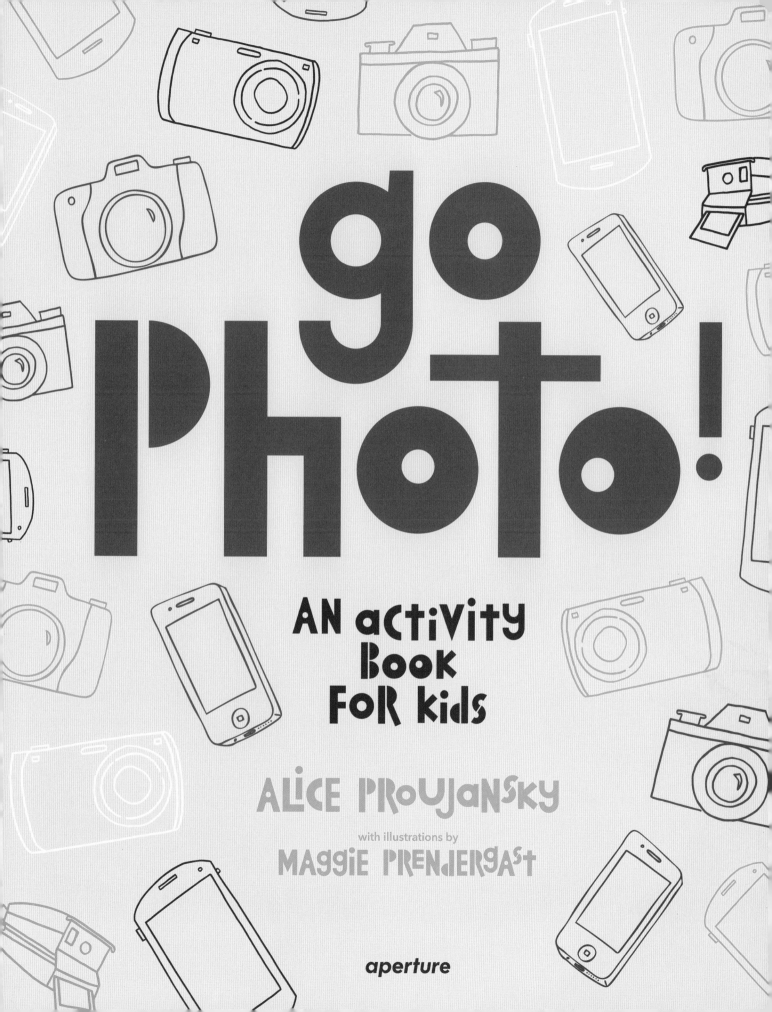

go photo!

AN activity Book FoR kids

ALiCE PROUJaNSKY

with illustrations by

MAGGiE PRENJERGASt

aperture

let's do this!

FUN RULES

Welcome to *Go Photo!* This book contains activities that you can do alone, with friends, or with an adult. All you need is yourself and a camera (any camera), and you're ready to go! Here are some rules, but feel free to skip them and just start on any activity now. You can come back here when you have questions or want a break from taking photos!

TAKE LOTS OF PICTURES

Oops! Your mom's eyes were closed. Whoa, a bird just flew by! Darn, your brother just photobombed your picture. The more photographs you take of a situation, the more likely you are to get a good one, and the more interesting things you'll notice. You can't take too many photos. Just go!

DON'T GET CAUGHT UP IN THE TECHNICAL STUFF

Use whatever camera you have. You don't need fancy equipment to take great photographs. You will need to be able to print pictures in most of these activities, but don't worry if you're out of photo paper, or if you don't have poster board to glue them to. Use regular paper; find a shoebox, an old notebook cover, a folder, or some cardboard. Improvise. Don't let the stuff get in the way of the fun. That said, if you want to make the final products nicer (maybe you're making that photo mask as a gift), you might want to get real photo paper or send the prints off to be printed professionally by an online service.

DECIDE WHAT GOES IN THE PICTURE

What you include in a picture and what you don't include is a choice. When you're taking a picture, look carefully at what is inside the frame (the 4 edges that surround the photograph) and think about where you're placing things within that frame. What is the subject or main idea of your picture? Should it be in the center of the frame? Or off to the side? What is in the background of your picture? What is cut off or left out of the frame? Think about the whole picture, including the edges and corners, not just the middle. Think about leaving something out. Think about including something extra. Be creative and play around as you make these decisions.

MOVE AROUND

Where you stand and where you hold the camera determine what is in the photograph just as much as when you press the button. Move the camera around to get everything in the right place, to include more (or less) of the background, or to change the point of view. Your point of view changes the way things look. Holding the camera way down below your subject (making the camera look "up" at your subject) will make it look bigger, important, or intimidating. This is called a worm's-eye view. You can also photograph something from the opposite point of view, by holding your camera way above your subject to make it look small or unimportant. This is called a bird's-eye view.

BE STILL

At the same time, when your body moves, the camera moves, and moving the camera too much when you push the button can make your photographs blurry (especially when there isn't a lot of light, like indoors or in the evening). Try to stand as still as you can when you take the photo. If your photographs look blurry, make yourself very steady: stand with your feet spread slightly apart, brace your arms against your body, and hold your breath as you take the picture. You can also make a miniature stand to hold your iPod or smartphone camera steady while you use the self-timer (see page 9).

ZOOM WITH YOUR FEET

Most cameras have a zoom feature that makes the pictures look like you're closer to your subject than you really are. This is tempting to use, especially when you don't want to get too close to your subject, like with a stranger or lava. But standing far away and using zoom to take a photo makes the pictures lower quality. So try moving closer to your subject instead. (Unless your subject is, in fact, lava. Then use the zoom.)

go to THE LighT

Light is what makes the image show up in the photograph, so pay attention to where the light is shining and move toward it. Our eyes are much better at seeing in dim light than our cameras are. Make your camera happy by feeding it enough good light to avoid blurry, low-quality photographs. Usually, light looks best in the early morning or early evening, when shadows are long and the sunlight turns golden. Midday light can be a bright, harsh, even mean light. You can work with that kind of light, if you need to, or else try photographing in shade, if you are out between about 10:00 a.m. and 2:00 p.m. Keep in mind, it's better to take a picture with the sun or light source behind you and your camera. If you photograph toward the sun, your subject may show up as a dark shadow in your picture, since the camera adjusts to all the light behind it. You need light, but you don't want your camera to be blinded by the light. That said, feel free to play around with using the light in different ways—maybe you want your subject to be a shadow!

READ THE diRECTiONS FiRSt

When doing a *Go Photo!* activity, it helps to read the directions and tips all the way through before starting. Then you won't get halfway through and discover you are missing something essential (like sidewalk chalk, a box, or a glass of water). However, if you do find you are missing something, don't panic; you can almost always improvise (see Fun Rule #2: Don't Get Caught Up in the Technical Stuff).

ASk FoR HELP

Some of these activities include downloading photographs from your camera and printing them, climbing a ladder, or making a robot. Go ahead and ask an older kid or adult for help any time you need it. There are also activities that call for printing pictures at a certain size or with multiple pictures on a sheet of paper. If it's not obvious how to do this in the print dialog box (the one that comes up when you hit "print"), look up the directions online for the software you're using or ask for help.

SaVE yOUR WORK

It's really disappointing when you lose all of your photographs because your camera falls in a lake. So save your files on a computer often. This way you can reprint your photos whenever you want—like, if you want to make a fancier version of one of your *Go Photo!* projects, or if a project didn't turn out quite right, and you want to try it again.

TURN OFF THE FLASH

Turn off the flash unless you really, really want it on. The flash gives you more light, but it also makes your pictures look different and can create harsh reflections on shiny surfaces. Try experimenting without the flash first. Then with the flash, too. Think about it as a choice rather than something you leave on by default.

MAKE it YOURS

These activities are ideas, but, of course, you have ideas, too. So if you think these would be better if you did them standing on your head, then stand right on your head. Or, try them while walking on a tightrope or wearing a cape. For a lot of these activities, you can use the ideas to take creative pictures without actually making the stuff. On the other hand, you can always print out the pictures even when the activity doesn't call for it and make a book (see pages 60–61) or put on a spontaneous photo exhibition on your fridge. Plus, these activities can be done again and again in different ways with different results!

How to MAKE a SMART PHONE STAND

For iPod or smartphone cameras, you can make a small stand to hold the camera to take selfies or action shots of yourself. You'll need 2 binder clips and a piece of cardboard.

1 Cut the cardboard to about the size of a business card or gift card (or better yet, use a business card or gift card!).

2 Clip the binder clips to each end of the card.

3 Place the stand on a stable surface.

4 Place your phone or iPod into the clip-cradle formed on top.

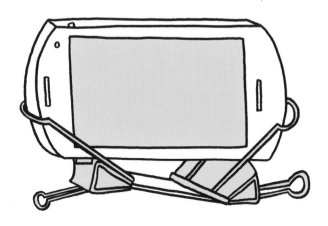

SCAVENGER HUNT

SCAVENGER HUNT

Let's get warmed up! Go on a photography scavenger hunt on your own or with a few friends. Look around the room or wherever you are right now. There are a million potential pictures in here, and everyone will choose different photos to take. Which ones do you want to take? How do you see? What do you notice that others don't? Take your time and get creative. Find at least 10 items on the list. Pay attention to the angle you choose for each picture, where you stand when you take it, and what you include in the frame.

stuff you'll need:

- [ ] Camera
- [ ] A few friends (optional)
- [ ] **30 minutes**

12

A triangle

Something bumpy

let's do this!

On your own or with some friends, go off and see if you can photograph all of these things. But don't take pictures of pictures; come on, that's boring!

Things on a table

— Something bumpy
— Something gross
— Something beautiful
— A triangle
— An oval
— A sphere
— A rectangle within a rectangle
— A lot of blue
— A tiny bit of blue
— A reflection
— Your shadow on 2 different surfaces
— Things on a table
— Flowing water
— A landscape
— Happiness (bonus points for shooting this without showing a face)
— Frustration
— Rest
— Speed
— Friendship
— Multiple people jumping in the air to do a high five (as many as possible, but at least 2)

Something beautiful

A tiny bit of blue

Rest

TIPS

The "frame" means the 4 edges that surround or "frame" the image that you photograph. Before taking a photo of a scavenger hunt object, think about where you are going to hold your camera, since its position will then frame the object. Be creative in how you set up your camera so that it frames the scavenger hunt objects in fun ways.

Have each friend add 1 item to the list or make up your own.

Look at your friends' pictures at the end to see how they differ.

Friendship

CAMERA oBSCuRa RoBot HEAD

Ready, set, go, and make your own camera, called a camera obscura, that you can wear on your head. Inside the camera obscura, you will see an image (like a photo!) of the world behind you. A camera obscura is a light-proof box with a small hole, called a "pinhole," that lets in a little bit of bright sunlight. Sunlight reflects off of objects outside the box, and when these rays of light travel through the pinhole, they cross each other and project an upside-down image of the outside world, inside the camera obscura. It sure looks like magic is happening inside the box, but ladies and gentlemen, this is real life! This is also how cameras and eyes work.

stuff you'll need:

- [ ] Cardboard box (big enough to fit your head in)
- [ ] Scissors
- [ ] Pencil
- [ ] White paper
- [ ] Paper plate
- [ ] Packing tape (preferably brown or black) or duct tape
- [ ] Markers, construction paper, and art supplies
- [ ] Dark-colored sweatshirt, T-shirt, scarf, or fabric
- [ ] Sunny day
- [x] **1 hour to an hour and a half**

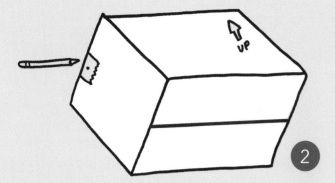

let's do this!

1. Leave the top of the box open and make sure the bottom is taped shut.

2. Along the edge of the bottom of the box, on one of the short sides, find the center (no need for a ruler—just estimate as best you can) and put a dot with a pencil here so that you can see where the center is. Then directly below the center point, poke a small hole (called a "pinhole") 1 to 2 inches from the bottom of the box that's about this big: ⟋

3. On the side opposite the pinhole, tape the white paper inside the box. Cover the whole side. This is your "screen" for your camera, the place where you will get to see the image of the outside world after the light comes through the pinhole.

4. Now you're going to make a hole for your head so that you can wear your camera obscura. Close the top of the box. Use a paper plate and pencil to trace a circle that's big enough for your head to go through. Make sure you trace on both sets of cardboard flaps, inner and outer.

5. Cut along the traced circle on both sets of flaps to make the hole.

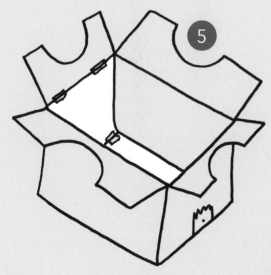

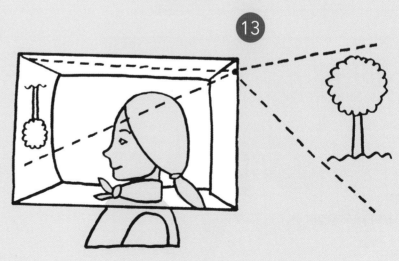

2

3

4

6 Look around inside of your box to find any light leaking through the cardboard. Tape up any leaks, layering the tape on the outside, if needed, so that the only light coming into the box is from the pinhole.

7 Using some art supplies, decorate the box to look like a terrifying/wonderful/world-dominating robot. Just make sure you don't cover the pinhole!

8 Put on the dark-colored sweatshirt or T-shirt without your arms in the sleeves, so it is just around your neck—wear it like a scarf. You can also use a dark-colored scarf or fabric. Now . . .

9 Put the box on so that the pinhole is behind your head.

10 Go outside.

No, wait! Go outside, and *then* put the camera obscura on your head with the hole at the back! No crashing into walls here.

11 Tuck your "scarf" in between your neck and the box, even up into the robot head, so no light leaks into the box.

12 Make sure your head isn't blocking the light coming through the pinhole.

13 Stand so that the sun is behind you.

You will now see an image of whatever is behind you—trees, buildings, cars, people, etc.—projected on the inside of the box.

TIPS

If you can't see the projection clearly, make the pinhole slightly bigger, and make sure no light is leaking into the box.

Make sure the sun is really shining brightly and that you're facing away from it.

Try taking a picture of the projection inside the box.

Robots HaVE FEELiNgs

Unfortunately, your all-powerful camera obscura robot head has one flaw. We're so sorry, but it was accidentally made with a full set of human emotions, despite the single facial expression you gave it. Your job here is to figure out how to photograph the robot's emotions without relying on the face. How can you use posture, pose, and gestures to communicate a mood?

stuff you'll need:

☐ Camera obscura robot head

☐ Camera

☐ Friend or adult helper

☐ **15 minutes**

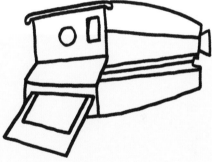

let's do this!

1 Put on the robot head.

2 Use your body to show the robot feeling terrified. Would it stand up straighter? Cower in fear? Cover its robot head with its robot arms?

3 Now try showing an overjoyed robot. Maybe its robot batteries were just charged! What would it do with its arms? Fist pump? High five? Now think about the legs. Is the robot jumping in the air? Doing a split? A victory dance?

4 Now use your body to show other emotions: sad, bored, silly, irritated, sleepy, whatever you want your robot to feel!

5 Have a friend or adult helper take a picture of you playing out each emotion of your robot.

TIPS

Think about your body language. How can the placement of your head or even your hands convey a feeling? If you get stuck, think about the exaggerated ways that cartoon characters show their emotions: droopy backs, worried fists clutched to the chest, hands grabbing heads in disbelief.

If you're doing this activity with a friend, you and the friend can take turns. First, you wear the robot head and your friend takes the photos of your robot emotions, and then your friend wears the robot head, and you take the photos.

Suggestion: Make sure to talk like a robot during this activity.

SELFiE FeSt

SELFIE FEST

There's lots more you can do with the selfie than you would ever guess. Here is a menu of creative ideas that go beyond taking a selfie of your face. Try to take as many of these selfies as you can. Liberal use of the self-timer is allowed.

stuff you'll need:

- [ ] Camera
- [ ] Yourself
- [ ] The world
- [ ] **5 minutes to an hour, depending**

let's do this!

Me all the time: Take a selfie at the same time every day for a week, a month, or a year.

Shadow: Capture your shadow on a textured surface like a brick wall or grass.

Reflection: Photograph your face reflected on still water, a computer screen, car window, or other reflective surface.

Infinity: Photograph yourself standing between 2 mirrors so it looks like there are endless copies of you.

Can you hair me? Take a picture with someone else's hair draped over your head.

Body parts: Photograph only parts of yourself. For example, show your hand holding a baseball or your feet in a stream.

Tiny bits: Take close-ups of your eyelashes, fingerprints, toenails, etc.

Face lift: Use clear tape to tape parts of your face in different directions. Make your nose look piggy or your eyebrows high and surprised.

Turn that frown upside-down: Hang your head over the side of a bed upside-down and take a selfie. To take it further, rest glasses on your chin, and cover your face from the nose down with a T-shirt or cloth.

All together now: Take a selfie-style picture of your whole family.

Action: Use the self-timer on your camera to catch a picture as you run/jump/swim/fly by.

Meet the feet: Take selfies of your shoes and feet. Show your shoes on cool floors. Photograph your feet on all the surfaces they meet in a day.

Bookie: Find a book with a face on its cover; hold it in front of you so it looks like the book's face is on your body.

Glamour: Get fancy! Dress up, do your hair, wear some makeup, if that's your thing.

Mirror mirror: Draw stuff on the mirror using dry-erase markers (more hair? An extra eye? Bird on the head?) and then photograph yourself in the drawing.

Dancer: Put on some music, set your camera's self-timer to go off every 10/15/20 seconds, and go nuts.

Traces in places: Photograph the traces your body leaves on the world: footprints, the shape left after lying in sand, or squished sofa cushions you just sat on.

Go Photo! Wear the Photo Face Masks (pages 34–35); pose with your Little Me (pages 30–31); smile in your Chalk Dreams drawing (pages 68–69); and photograph yourself through Mystery Photo filters (pages 38–39).

TIP For a quick and easy way to make a stand to hold a camera when using the self-timer, see page 9.

Exquisite Mix-Up

Exquisite Mix-Up

Great news! You invent a shrinking machine to shrink your friends and family. Bad news: it malfunctions, and your family's body parts get mixed up in ridiculous ways. In this Exquisite Mix-up you create a book of photos of your friends and family, and then mix and match the parts with each other. You could see your brother's curly hair with your dad's big feet and your mother's scrubs and stethoscope.

stuff you'll need:

- [ ] Camera
- [ ] At least 4 friends and/or family members
- [ ] Computer and printer
- [ ] Photo paper
- [ ] Stapler
- [ ] Scissors
- [ ] **45 minutes**

26

2

let's do this!

1 Choose a place that will be the background for the photos. You should choose a neutral background, like the side of your house or a wall in your house.

2 In front of your background, take a vertical photo of a person with the top of his or her head right at the top of the frame (but don't cut off the hair!) and his or her feet right at the bottom of the frame. Make sure the person is directly in the middle of the frame, looking straight at you, and has his or her hands at his or her sides.

3 Take more vertical photos in the same way and against the same background with at least 4 people.

Now that you have the pictures, assemble them.

4 Print the photos all the same size on separate sheets of photo paper.

5 Decide the order you want the people to appear in your book, and then stack the photos in that order.

6 Staple the photos together on the left edge to make a book. Use your scissors and cut away the white border of the page first, if you don't want a border around your photos.

7 Now make a cut through the whole stack of photos at the shoulder line (right below where the neck meets the shoulders), and then make a second cut just above where the hands are on the first person in the stack.

8 Turn 1 page at a time to mix and remix the parts into mixed-up mini people.

TIP

Vertical means holding the camera this way.

6

7

LiTTLE ME

What if you had a shrinking machine and could shrink yourself? How would everything look if you were super small? How would a change in size help you notice different things? Guess what? You do have a shrinking machine: the camera and your printer. Here, you create an action shot of yourself, print it out, attach it to a stick, and take your "Little Me" on a photographic adventure where ordinary objects become giant. You can go places that were impossible before. Everyday things take on new uses, while others become a major threat to humanity.

stuff you'll need:

- [ ] Camera
- [ ] Self-timer on a camera or a friend to take the photographs
- [ ] Computer and printer
- [ ] Glue
- [ ] Photo paper
- [ ] Poster board
- [ ] Scissors
- [ ] Tape
- [ ] Popsicle stick, pencil, or other stick-like item (or an actual stick!)
- [ ] **1 hour**

let's do this!

1 Use the self-timer on your camera (or a friend) to take a vertical photo of yourself so you fill up the frame. Make a shocked and horrified face! Make bold gestures with your arms and legs! Take a few more pictures with different expressions or actions.

2 Print out your favorite image on photo paper. Make sure not to print it too small or it will be difficult to cut out. Feel free to print out more than one!

3 Glue it to the poster board.

4 Cut out the mounted photo carefully, around the edges of your body (you don't want to cut off a foot by accident).

5 Tape the cut-out photo to the popsicle stick or other stick-like item to finish a Little Me.

6 Make more Little Mes if you like.

   Now let's take some pictures . . .

7 Take Little Me on adventures to some of the places you ordinarily hang out and see what kind of trouble Little Me can get into. Everything looks so strange to Little Me. A garden you used to walk by is now a jungle. That lazy, old dog is now a mouthful of teeth. Take lots of pictures along the way.

8 Try putting Little Me in nature or bring it to dinner. What does this Little Me eat? And what happens when Little Me encounters your food? Does it get tangled in spaghetti? Does it build a fort out of your favorite snack? Get lost in the salad?

9 Want to keep going? Build a little world for your Little Me. Take a photograph of the sky, print it out, and glue it to a cardboard or poster board background. Photograph a patch of grass, print it out, and glue it to the same backdrop. Keep going until you have made a diorama for the Little Me to live in.

TIPS

When making Little Me, big gestures work best. The more animated you are, the more emotion your Little Me will express. Be dramatic!

Little Me could play some great pranks. Try taking funny pictures of Little Me using your brother's toothbrush as a comb or piloting your cousin's LEGO helicopter or photobombing someone.

Once you're done with Little Me, you can remove the stick and use Little Me as a funny bookmark.

PHoto
FaCe MaSK

PHoto FaCE MasK

You know what would be funny? If you had a moustache! Or, if you had giant hair, or lots of wrinkles, or big sunglasses. Make and wear a mask of someone else's—or something else's—face.

stuff you'll need

- [ ] Camera
- [ ] Friends and family
- [ ] Computer and printer
- [ ] Photo paper
- [ ] Poster board or cardstock (optional)
- [ ] Glue (optional)
- [ ] Scissors
- [ ] Popsicle stick, pencil, or other stick-like item (or an actual stick!)
- [ ] Tape
- [ ] **30 minutes**

let's do this!

1. Take a picture of a friend or family member's face. Hold the camera close to the person's face so that you fill the frame with the face, but be sure not to crop the hair. If possible, have your person wear a hat. Or, if you want to make a mask of your own face, have someone take your picture. Or, if you want an animal mask, you could take a picture of your pet's face.

2. Print out your photograph on photo paper. Generally, the picture should fill a whole page to make a mask. Try a test print on regular paper first to determine if you need to print the picture larger or smaller. You can see if it will fit as a mask by holding the test print up to your face for size. Print the image again, if needed, and adjust the size by using the scale function in the print dialog box of your software (the one that comes up when you hit "print"). To make the picture bigger, type in a higher percentage (like 110 percent); to make it smaller, try it at 85 percent. Continue to adjust as needed. It might take 1 or 2 tests for the perfect fit.

3. Cut out the face, carefully following the outline of the shape.

4. Cut off the bottom of the face. This way the mask will still show the wearer's nose, mouth, and chin. Leave the cheeks attached, but cut away space for a nose. (OK, this is sounding very gruesome. Sorry!) If you're making a pet mask, leave the nose and mouth intact.

5. Poke small eyeholes where the pupils are by using a pencil point. This way you will be able to see when you're wearing the mask.

6. Turn the mask over and place the stick or pencil on 1 side. Tape it down.

7. Hold the mask in front of your face. Wear it with pride! Take a selfie in it.

TIPS

To make the mask stronger, glue the photo to poster board before you cut it out or just print it on cardstock, if you have it.

You could also make a mask out of the bottom of the face (it would be fun to find someone with a beard or a pointy moustache). In this case, cut around and tape the bottom half of the face (just below the nose) to a stick or pencil. Repeat Step 7.

MYSTERY PHOTOS

MYSTERY PHOTOS

Make any photo more mysterious—without a
computer—by using different materials as filters to
shoot through.

stuff you'll need:

- [ ] Camera
- [ ] Semi-transparent things:
  a glass of water, etc.,
  or things with holes: a
  straw, etc.
- [ ] **30 minutes**

let's do this!

1   Walk through your home (or school, or garage, or backyard) and collect items that could be used as filters: objects that are semi-transparent (partly see-through), like bubble wrap, pool toys, or a glass of lemonade. Shooting through items with small holes, like a net or through a tube, also works great.

2   Hold a filter in front of your camera lens and take photographs of different objects through it. How does the filter change the look of a solid color? Of a person? Of a plant?

3   Try using the flash on your camera and holding a colorful filter over the flash. You can also take a photograph holding the filter over both the flash and the lens of your camera. This activity works best in the dark.

4   Keep on going! Keep finding more filters! Keep photographing more objects through your filters! When will we stop? Never! Onward and upward, photo-humans!

TIP   Almost any object that you can see through can be a filter. Try taking photographs through sunglasses, a rainy window, colored plastic, lace, gauze, a scarf, a star-shaped hole cut out of cardboard, a magnifying glass, a pair of tights—the list is endless.

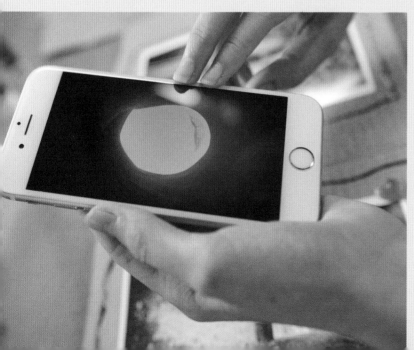

7:30

8:30

10:30

11:30

PHOTO TIME

9:30

12:30

PHoTo tiME

It's easy to take a beautiful picture of a sunset! But what if you didn't get to plan when or where to take pictures? Could you find an interesting photograph no matter where you were? Set a series of alarms and photograph something interesting no matter where you are each time the alarm rings. You can do this activity by yourself, or with a friend to see how 2 people photograph the same place at the same time of day differently.

stuff you'll need:

☐ Camera

☐ Friend (optional)

☐ Alarm

☐ **30 minutes to 2 hours, depending**

42

let's do this!

1 Choose a time when you'll have the camera and alarm with you and can make some noise. Use the alarm on your smartphone or iPod, if you have one. You don't want to do this one in class or during an undercover spy mission!

2 Set the alarm to go off at least 5 times during the time you'll be photographing. If you're with a friend, have your friend set alarms for the same times. Could be every 5 minutes or every 2 hours. It's up to you.

3 When the alarm goes off, stop right in your tracks and take a photograph. Don't rush. Take your time, and try and find something interesting or funny or beautiful around you, no matter where you are.

4 Repeat the process each time the alarm goes off.

5 When you're finished, look at your photos to see how you captured the world around you at different times of the day. If you're with a friend, compare photographs. What kinds of similarities between your photos do you see? What kinds of differences? Does one of you like photographing people? Does one of you always look down, or notice bright colors, or photograph shapes?

TIPS

You could make this activity last longer (set the alarms to go off over a whole day) or shorter (take a 15-minute walk and set the alarms to ring every 3 minutes during it).

Try doing this activity with a friend who lives far away to see what you were doing at the exact same time in 2 different places. You can text each other your photos at the end.

Test Sophistication
Room

PHoto DeTECTiVE

PHoto DETECTiVE

Here, you will think up an imaginary mystery, crime, or event, and spend your afternoon being a detective and documenting "evidence" you find with your camera: getaway cars, suspicious characters, and mysterious clues. Watch as the mystery you imagine changes how you see things and what you photograph.

stuff you'll need:

☐ Camera

☐ Friend or adult helper (optional)

☐ Computer and printer

☐ Photo paper

☐ **An afternoon**

let's do this!

1 Decide what imaginary mystery, crime, or event you're going to pretend happened: Is it a diamond heist? Evidence of an alien landing? Superheroes in disguise? Or recently discovered traces of a lost culture?

2 As you go through your afternoon, keep the story in mind. Look around for "clues" during your everyday activities, and photograph them. That's not just a car you see; it's a getaway car. That's not just a room; it's a crime scene or a hideout. The fingerprints on the water glass: clues. The mailman? A suspect or maybe a witness. Take photographs as you come across anything that could be part of your elaborate plot. You could also have a friend or a parent or adult helper pretend to be a suspicious character or witness. Take photographs of them doing things that relate to your imagined event.

3 Print your pictures out on photo paper, and create a crime or event investigation wall showing and connecting the dots between the who, what, where, when, and why of the plot. If you do this activity with a friend, discuss the mystery or the imagined event and how the clues fit together. If you want, go out and take more photos to add to the story.

TIPS

Working with a friend/detective partner is fun.

You could put all your photos together and make a book. See pages 60–61.

TELEPHONE GAME

TELEPHONE GAME

Have you ever played the telephone game? You whisper a phrase to a friend: "I like eggs and bacon." The friend whispers what she thinks she heard to someone else: "My right leg is shakin'." The next friend continues: "My fight egg was taken!" and so on. The farther the message travels, the weirder it gets. Here, you'll play the telephone game with the camera and then make a set of "photo-dominoes" out of the pictures to continue the game afterward.

stuff you'll need:

- [ ] Camera
- [ ] Bunch of friends
- [ ] Computer and printer
- [ ] Photo paper
- [ ] Scissors
- [ ] Glue (optional)
- [ ] Poster board (optional)
- [ ] Magazines or newspapers (optional)
- [ ] **1 hour**

50

let's do this!

Play the game and start the "conversation":

1 Take a picture of something, anything! That's easy enough; what could possibly go wrong?

2 Give the camera to a friend and ask her or him to look at the image and take another photograph, keeping *1* thing the same from your photograph—the same color, shape, texture, number, or subject.

3 Keep passing the camera along to more and more people (or hand it back and forth) until you have a series of photographs. When taking the photograph, each person must keep *1* thing the same as what was in the photo taken right before it. You never know where this will lead, and that's the fun of it.

Make the photo-dominoes:

4 Print out the series of photos onto photo paper, smallish—about 3 x 5 inches or less should create a good set to shuffle around. You can make the images smaller by setting them up to print multiple photos on a page. In this case, 4 on a page would work well for size. If it's not obvious how to print multiple images on 1 page in the print dialog box when you try to print, look up the directions online for the software you're using.

5 Cut them out. If you want to make sturdier cards, glue the pictures to poster board, and cut them out.

6 If you want to make more photo-dominoes, cut out pictures from newspapers and magazines. Again, make each photo relate to the photo right before it in the telephone line by keeping 1 thing the same.

7 Put all the photos on a table in the telephone line order (the photograph of a red strawberry next to one of a red hat, which is next to one of a wig, which is next to one of a willow tree that droops like long hair, and so on).

8 Mix them up, and make a new sequence using some of the same grouping principles (color, number, subject)!

TIPS

This game is fun to play while you take a walk.

A sequence is a series of photographs put in an order that creates relationships between photos and changes their meaning. A photo can mean one thing alone, but it can mean something totally different when placed next to another photo. With your friends or on your own, try making different pairs and sequences that change the meaning of a photo.

TREaSURE HUNt

X

TREaSURE HUNt

How can you use photography to make a mystery and solve it? Hide a treasure and create photo-clues that lead back to it. Then give a friend clues to solve the mystery and find the hidden treasure.

stuff you'll need

- [ ] Camera
- [ ] Friend
- [ ] Treasure or something special or funny to hide
- [ ] Paper and pen
- [x] **30 minutes**

let's do this!

1. Hide the treasure.

2. Choose a starting point for the treasure hunt, knowing that you'll be walking to the hiding place and photographing the landmarks you see along the way to use as clues. Be sure to choose a starting point that will help create a path with some twists, turns, and detours before coming to the treasure.

3. Stand at the starting point and look around for a landmark on your route that you can photograph as the first clue. Be sure to pick something that you can see from the starting point. Photograph the landmark or object that you have chosen. This is Clue #1.

4. Standing next to Clue #1, look around and pick something that you can see as the second clue. Walk over and take a picture of it for Clue #2. Now continue to take photographs of more clues on the path to the treasure. Make sure the second clue is within view of the first clue, the third clue is within view of the second, and so on. Keep taking photos of clues until you are close enough to have the hiding place in sight (at least 5 clues, but probably no more than 10). This adds an element of "I Spy" to the hunt, and the photo-clues will help your friend stay on track.

5. Don't take a photograph of the last location—the hiding place—that would be way too easy! Instead, write down a hint and photograph the note as the last clue. This way the treasure-hunter can't just look at the last picture and find the treasure; they must follow your path instead!

   Now, you're ready for your friend to find the treasure.

6. Set up your photos on your camera so that the first photo is Clue #1.

7. Hand the camera over to your friend and ask him or her to look at the photos, one by one, and follow the path of clues to the hidden treasure. Your friend should only look at the pictures of the clues in order.

TIPS

Take turns with a friend. First, you hide a treasure and photograph the clues leading to it, and then your friend hides a treasure and makes the photo-clues.

If you and your friend are using iPods or smartphones, the "treasure hider" can start off by texting the first clue. When the "treasure hunter" finds Clue #1, they can text their own photo of it back in order to receive the next clue.

The clues can be landmarks that literally point in the direction of the next clue. Like, a curvy tree branch could point in the direction of the next clue: a big, red barn.

Faces in Places

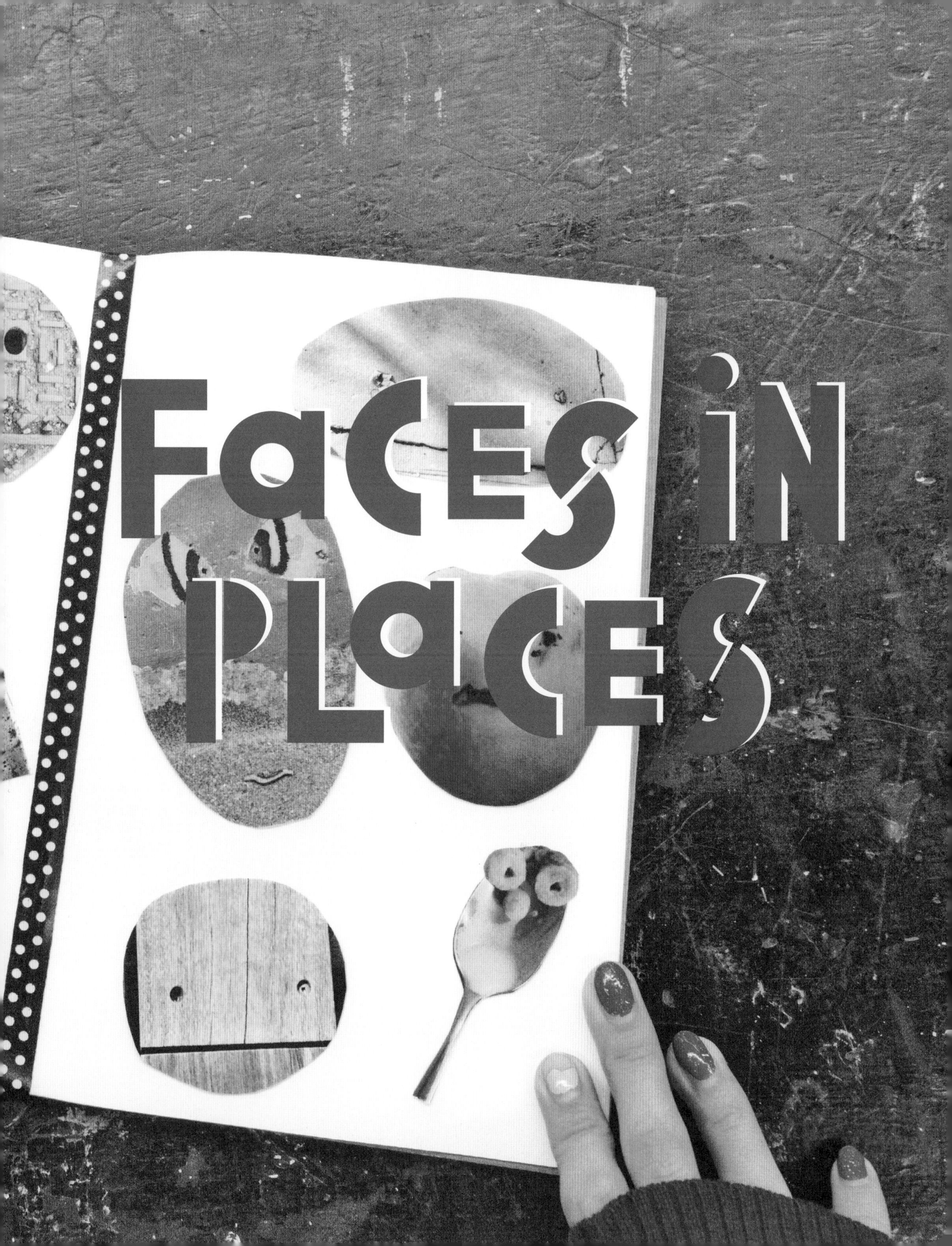

FaCES iN PLaCES

People are very sensitive to images of the human face, which can explain why we are so likely to see patterns in the world that resemble faces. Use your camera to capture some face patterns you see in the world around you, and create your own smiley stickers.

stuff you'll need:

- [ ] Camera
- [ ] Computer and printer
- [ ] Sticker paper (letter-size)
- [ ] Scissors
- [x] **1 hour**

let's do this!

1 Look around very closely for anything that looks like a face. (Well, except for actual faces. Too easy!)

2 Get to photographing. Grumpy-looking peach? Take a photograph. Dresser with knobs for eyes and a drawer for a mouth? Done. Trees are easy—all those faces in the bark. Fire hydrants, faucets, sidewalk cracks, food, flowers, cars. Pretty soon it seems like faces are glowering, cackling, sneering, and grinning everywhere.

3 When you have a lot of photographs exposing the previously hidden faces that lurk all around, print them onto sticker paper. This works best when you print multiple photos onto 1 sheet of letter-sized sticker paper. Depending on how big you want your stickers to be, try printing 4 to 9 photos per page. Just make sure you put the sticker paper into your printer instead of the regular paper that's already in there.

4 Cut circles around each image to make them face-shaped, and now you have a series of photo-face stickers!

TIPS

Don't be afraid to cut out different shapes or to draw more facial features (like googly eyes) onto your stickers to make the expressions more pronounced, and fun!

Wear a different photo-face sticker on your shirt every day for a week.

Make a blank book (next page), and fill it with photo-face stickers.

How to MAKE A BLANK Book

Here you will make a blank book to put photographs (or anything!) in. You can use this for saving photos from any *Go Photo!* activity. Also, when you come to activities with "book" in the title (Rainbow Book, Accordion Picture-Poem Book, Action Flip-Book) you can skip making the book described in those activities, if you want, and just use this blank book instead.

stuff you'll need:

- [ ] Paper
- [ ] Thin cardboard (poster board, folder, or cereal box)
- [ ] Scissors
- [ ] Ruler
- [ ] Stapler
- [ ] String (optional)
- [ ] **15 minutes**

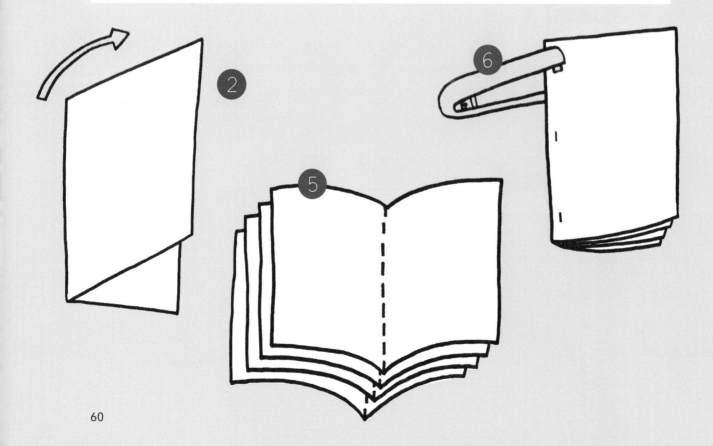

let's do this!

1. Place several sheets of regular paper on top of each other neatly. About 5 pieces of paper should work. If you use too many pieces of paper, the book starts to get sloppy.

2. Fold the stack of paper in half, and smooth down the folded edge very firmly.

   Now, for the cover.

3. Cut out a piece of cardboard so it's the same size as the paper. This will be the front and back cover of your book.

4. Next, you will want to fold the cardboard in half so that it can wrap around the stack of paper. To make the cardboard easier to fold, drag the tip of the scissors straight down the middle of the cardboard where the half-fold should be—without cutting all the way through. This is called "scoring." You can guide the scissors-blade by placing a ruler where you want the fold, and running the scissors-blade alongside the ruler.

5. Put the folded paper stack inside of the folded cardboard to make a book shape.

   Now you will make the binding, which will hold your book together.

6. To bind your book, staple the spine (the folded edge) in 3 places, so the longer smooth edges of the staples face up.

7. If you want to make a nicer binding: Open your book to the middle page so it lays flat on the table. Take a piece of string and tie it around the middle where the fold is—and what will be the spine—of the book. (Ask someone to place a finger on the string while you are tying the knot to keep it tight.) Move the bow to the outside of the cover afterward.

8. Add your own contents!

7

Rainbow Book

RaiNbow Book

Catch a rainbow in a book. Look for things that are the same color, photograph them, and arrange them into a collage rainbow book.

stuff you'll need:

- [ ] Camera
- [ ] Computer and printer
- [ ] Photo paper
- [ ] Paper to make a blank book
- [ ] Scissors
- [ ] Glue
- [ ] Newspapers/magazines/catalogues (optional)
- [ ] Markers or crayons (optional)
- [ ] **2 to 3 hours**

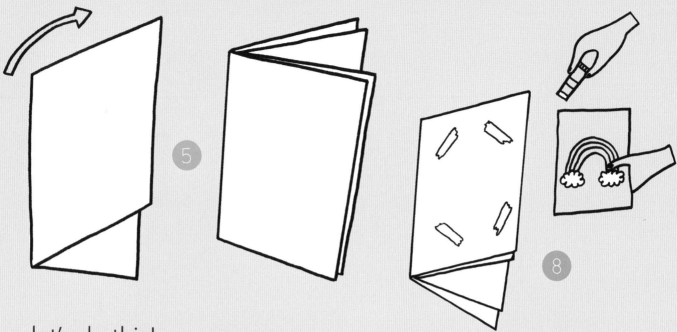

let's do this!

1. Photograph at least 5 red things. Very red! All kinds of shades of red.

2. Photograph at least 5 orange things. Very orange! All kinds of shades of orange.

3. Photograph at least—alright, alright, you see where this is headed. Continue photographing until you have at least 5 photographs for each color in the rainbow: red, orange, yellow, green, blue, and purple.

4. Using a printer, print out the photographs in color on photo paper.

5. Take 2 sheets of regular paper together and fold them in half to create a "book" with enough pages for each color and a cover, too. (Or if you want to make a nicer blank book, see pages 60-61 for directions.)

6. Open to page 1 (left page) and glue all of your red photos onto that. You can cut them up and collage them, or put the whole photographs in.

7. On page 2 (right page), glue on all your orange photographs (cut up, collage, or just the whole photographs). Continue until you have 1 page of photographs for each color.

8. If you want, create a rainbow design on the front cover using markers or crayons, or leftover photos that you didn't put in the book.

TIP If you want more photos to fill the pages, cut out images from newspapers, magazines, or catalogues and add them to your rainbow book.

CHALK dREAMS

CHALK dREAMS

Photography is great at showing the things we can see, but how can you make a photograph show invisible things, like your wishes or dreams? Here, you will use sidewalk chalk to draw a place you wish to see or a place that you've always dreamt about seeing. The place can be real or imaginary. Then you will travel to that place in the photograph!

stuff you'll need

- [ ] Camera
- [ ] Friend
- [ ] Adult helper
- [ ] Blacktop, concrete, or sidewalk
- [ ] Sidewalk chalk
- [ ] Ladder
- [ ] **1 hour**

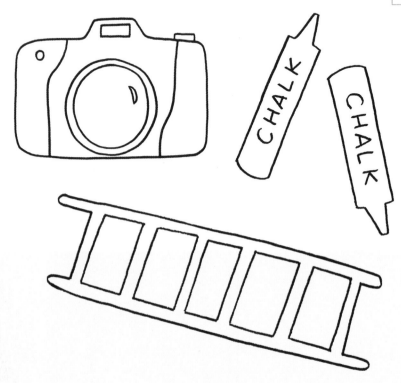

68

let's do this!

1 Talk to and dream with your friend about ideas for a place you want to draw and then "visit" in a photograph. Where would you like to go together? What would you do there? Who would you be? Would you be astronauts in outer space? Superheroes flying through the clouds? Fairies on a tropical island?

2 Find some open space on your driveway, sidewalk, or the blacktop at a playground to make a chalk drawing. Using your sidewalk chalk, draw a large frame. Have your friend lie down in the area so you know how big the frame has to be. Then draw the frame around your friend and leave lots of extra space for you to lie down inside it, too. Also be sure to leave extra space for the background you will draw inside the frame.

3 Together, you and your friend now need to draw the background of the dream place, leaving space for both of you to lie down in the frame.

4 Lie down in the background together.

5 Have an adult helper climb high enough on a ladder to photograph you 2 from above.

TIP Make sure to include the whole drawing of the place in the photograph.

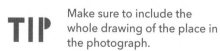

ACTioN FLip-Book

ACTION FLIP-BOOK

How can you recreate movement with still photographs? Take lots of pictures one after another, and make a flip-book. Flip-books work by showing us a series of photos more quickly than our brain can keep track of them; so our brain thinks it's seeing something that's moving, when everything is actually still. This is called stop-action photography.

stuff you'll need:

- [ ] Camera (with burst mode helpful, but not necessary)
- [ ] Friend who knows how to do a cartwheel (or other trick)
- [ ] Sunny location
- [ ] Computer and printer
- [ ] Photo paper
- [ ] Notebook, index cards, or sticky note notepad
- [ ] Scissors
- [ ] Glue stick
- [ ] Stapler or binder clip (if using index cards)
- [ ] **1 hour**

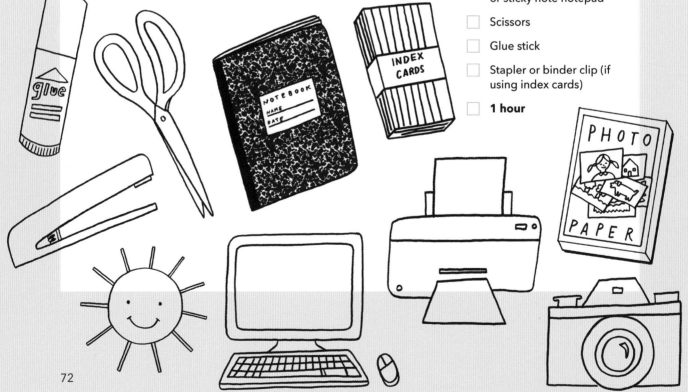

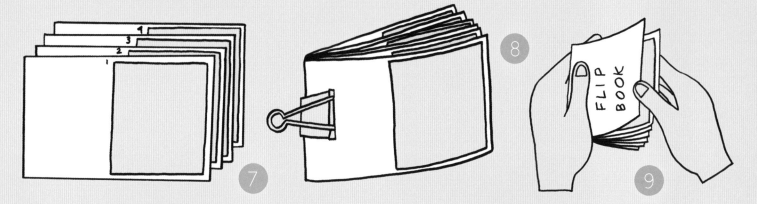

let's do this!

1   And . . . action! Head outside on a sunny day. (You don't want to accidentally kick over the fish tank in here.)

2   Find a background that's not too cluttered (a brick wall or grassy field is probably better and less distracting than, say, a circus). Bright sun works best so the photographs won't be blurry.

3   Start pressing the shutter button just before your friend starts a nice, slow cartwheel or other action. Hold the camera very still, facing straight ahead as he or she passes before you, and hold the button down so your camera takes a lot of pictures really quickly (this is called "burst mode" and is available on most cameras and phones). Don't let go until a few seconds after your friend is done. Make sure you have at least 15 to 20 pictures of the action.

4   Photograph 2 more cartwheels/actions in the same way, just to be sure you've got it. You can preview how the flip-book will work by looking through the photos you've taken very quickly on your camera's screen.

5   Print out the photographs on photo paper. Smaller-size photographs will work better in your flip-book than regular-size photos. You can make the images smaller by setting them up to print multiple photos on a page. In this case, 6 on a page would work well for size.

6   Number the photographs on the backside of the paper so they don't get jumbled up, and so you can remember what order they go in. Now, cut them out.

7   Glue the first photograph you took onto the first right-hand page of the notebook, with the photo's right edge touching the notebook's right edge. Or glue the photo onto the right edge of the index card or first page of the sticky note pad.

8   Turn the page (or go to the next index card). Repeat Step 7 with the second photograph you took. Continue with the photos until you have glued all of them into your book. If using the index cards, stack and staple or clip them together.

9   When the glue is dry, flip through the book quickly. It will look like your friend is cartwheeling (or doing some other trick) along the edge of the pages of the flip-book.

TIP   If your flip-book feels too short, print the whole set of pictures a second time, and glue it in after the first set. The motion might not flow perfectly, but you can think of it as a home-made GIF!

OUTSIDE-IN WALLPAPER

OUTsiDE-iN WALLPaPER

Capture your favorite view of the great outdoors through many small rows of pictures. Add all these bits together to re-create the scene indoors in a big, blocky wallpaper grid for your room.

stuff you'll need:

- [ ] Camera
- [ ] Computer and printer
- [ ] Photo paper
- [ ] Pen or pencil
- [ ] Scissors
- [ ] Double-sided or regular tape (parent-approved, that won't destroy the wall)
- [ ] Wall or place to tape up photos
- [ ] **About 2 to 3 hours**

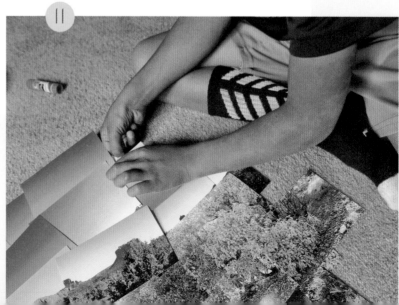

let's do this!

1. Find a beautiful, wide-open outdoor or indoor view that you like.

2. Using the zoom feature on your camera, zoom in on the scene, and then take a photograph of the details on the far left at the very top of the view.

3. Move the camera to the right a little bit, and take another photo. Make sure the right edge of the first photo overlaps with the left edge of the second one.

4. Keep going until you have photographed the top strip of the view from left to right. It'll probably take 5 photographs to do this.

5. Move the camera down a bit. Photograph another strip of the view, moving from right to left just underneath the strip you photographed last time. Make sure the top of these photos overlaps with the bottom of the first row.

6. Keep taking rows of photos like this until you've photographed the entire view.

7. Print out the photos (either 1 or 2 per page, so kinda large) onto photo paper, and using a pen or pencil, number them on the back in the order you took them. This will save you a lot of time and confusion in case they get mixed up!

8. Trim the pictures so there is no white border around them.

9. Keep them in their exact order, and arrange the photographs on the floor near the wall or place where you intend them to go.

10. Arrange the pictures together and overlap them where needed to get the scene to line up in a pleasing way. It's OK if the whole grid doesn't form a perfect rectangle; in fact, it's better if it doesn't.

11. Once you have the grid the way you want it, and while the pictures are still on the floor right-side-up, gently lift small sections of overlapping pictures and tape them together on the back. Continue this until you have different sections taped together.

12. Turn a section or row over, and apply double-sided tape (or loops of regular tape) to the back.

13. Stick the first section or row up on the wall.

14. Do the same thing, section by section, row by row, until the entire scene is on the wall.

TIPS The bigger your print-outs are, the better. Then the grid will be bigger, too.

This doesn't need to look perfect. Seriously! It's more interesting that way.

14

FRIENDSHiP tRiPTych

Here, you will take a series of pictures that represent a friendship without actually taking a picture of your friend's face. Can you take photographs that tell the story of your friendship? How can you take pictures that capture your friend's best qualities? What if we could see our memories outside of our heads? What would they look like? After you take your photos, you will choose 3 of them and create a triptych. Artists have been making triptychs (3 related images side by side) for over a thousand years. Now you can make your own modern triptych with your photos!

stuff you'll need:

- [ ] Camera
- [ ] Friend
- [ ] Pen and paper
- [ ] Computer and printer
- [ ] Photo paper
- [ ] Poster board, cardboard, or 3-part hinged frame, if you're fancy
- [ ] Glue stick
- [ ] Scissors
- [ ] Ruler
- [ ] Markers, construction paper, and art supplies
- [ ] **1 and a half hours**

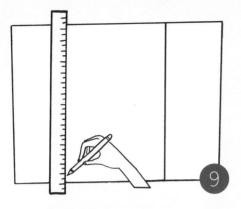

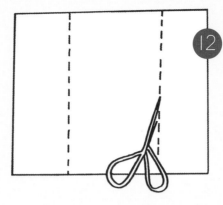

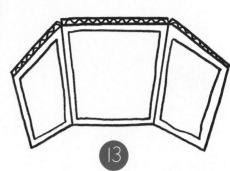

let's do this!

For the shoot:

1 Using a pen and paper, make a list with your friend of favorite things about your friendship. What do you like to do together? Where do you hang out? What do you have in common? How did you meet? What do you like about each other? Use this list for ideas of what to photograph. Important! Make sure you take all the photographs using the same orientation, either all vertical or all horizontal.

2 Now that you have your list, start photographing things off the list or related to the list. Your friend can also help you take the photographs. Photograph an object that shows 1 of your friend's talents. A paintbrush? A soccer ball? A unicycle?

3 Photograph a place that means something to the 2 of you. The room where you hatch plans or plot world domination; the park or field where you play sports; the tree where you meet up after school.

4 Make a portrait of your friend without showing his or her face. Feet covered in dirt from your explorations; hands holding a journal filled with thoughts; the back of his or her head covered with braids.

5 Photograph anything else that has meaning related to your friend or your friendship.

Make the triptych:

6 Look at all the photographs with your friend. Choose your 3 favorites.

7 Print the photos out on photo paper. You may want to print them out in a large size to fill up a good amount of space if you are using poster board or cardboard. At least 4 x 6 inches or larger, depending on the size you plan to make the triptych.

8 Line up the 3 photos next to each other on the poster board (or piece of cardboard or 3-part hinged frame) with room in between for decorating. Don't glue them down yet!

9 Cut the poster board or cardboard to the size of the 3 prints together. Leave some border space around each photo.

10 Use a glue stick to attach the photos to the board.

11 Decorate the frame around the pictures using construction paper, markers, and other art supplies.

12 Drag the tip of the scissors straight down the back of the board in between each photo without cutting all the way through–to help it bend better. This is called "scoring." You can guide the scissors-blade by placing a ruler where you want the fold, and running the scissors-blade alongside the ruler.

13 Bend the board inward where you made the scores with your scissors so your triptych will stand up.

TIPS Take a lot of pictures so you have lots of options when choosing your favorite photographs.

You can make this triptych as a gift for your friend or even a family member. Just keep it a surprise while you're photographing.

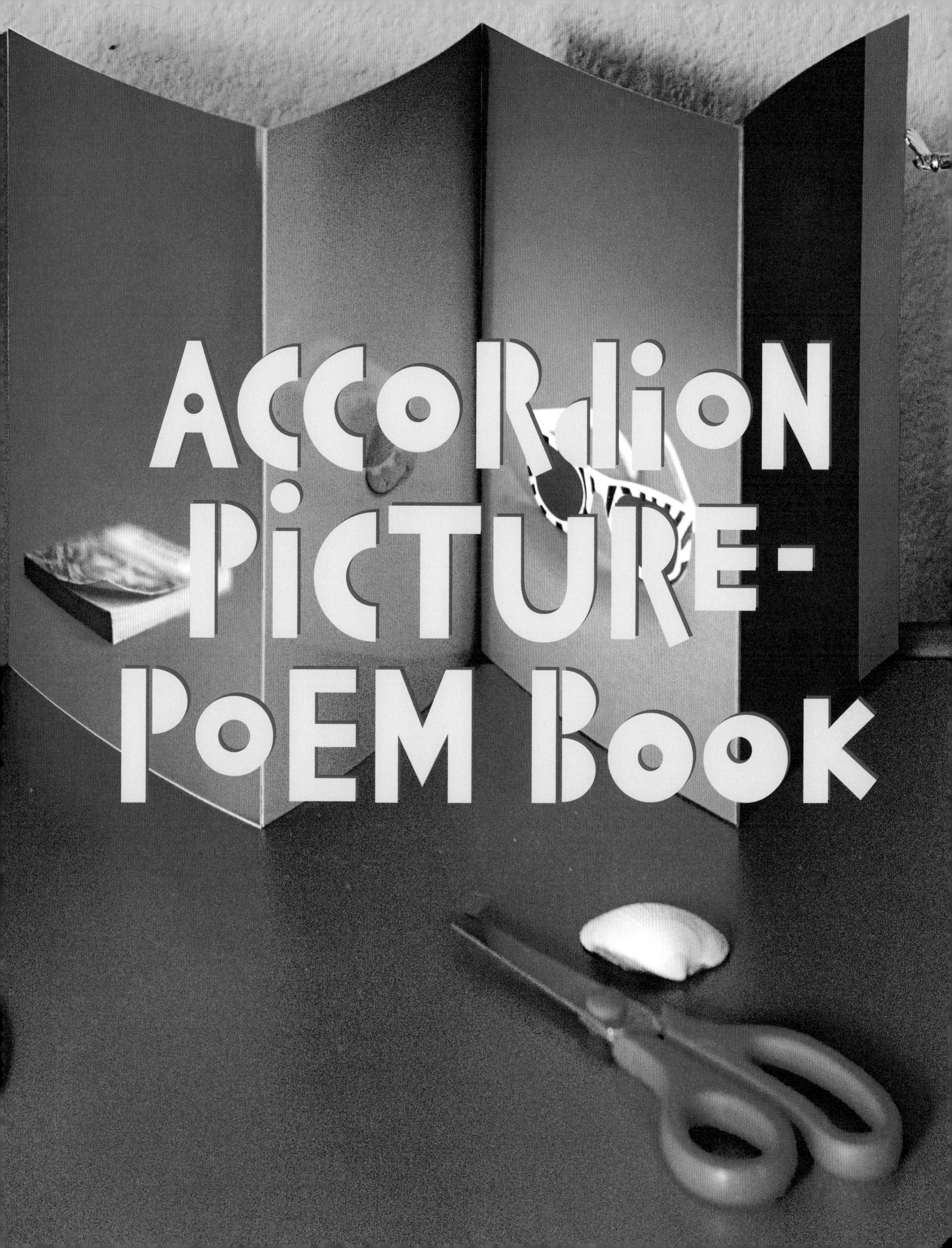
ACCORdion
PiCTURE-
PoEM Book

ACCORDiON PiCTURE-PoEM Book

Have you ever been to a place that you loved and wished you could make time stop there? Did you wish you could take all the fun things you saw at that special place back home with you? Here, you collect items from a place you love, photograph them in the style of a still life, and write mini-poems about them. You use photography and words together to try to capture the details of a special place in a picture-poem accordion book.

stuff you'll need:

- [ ] Camera
- [ ] Helper
- [ ] Favorite place
- [ ] At least 5 objects from the favorite place
- [ ] At least 5 different solid-colored backdrops (color poster boards, bedsheets, painted walls, etc.)
- [ ] Computer and printer
- [ ] Photo paper
- [ ] Scissors
- [ ] Tape
- [ ] Poster board
- [ ] Scraps of paper (in different colors)
- [ ] Pen or marker (bright or sparkly ones would be good)
- [ ] Glue
- [ ] Construction paper, and art supplies
- [ ] **2 hours**

84

let's do this!

Taking the photos:

1. Plan to do this when you're going to one of your favorite places. Let's say you're going to the beach for a weekend. Or, maybe you're going to summer camp. Or, to your crazy aunt's house for Thanksgiving. You get the idea.

2. Collect objects that tell the story of the place. We're talking seashells, a roller coaster ticket, mini-golf scorecard, or shark's tooth.

3. When you get home, take out the objects that you collected from your favorite place.

4. Now you need to make the backdrops for your photographs. Bend the colored poster board (or other backdrop) slightly, and put 1 object on top of it so you can only see the object and the colored background when you look through the camera. By doing this, you are creating a beautiful, solid color background for each of your special objects. You'll probably need a relative or friend to help hold the backdrop while you photograph the object on it.

5. Take a vertical photograph that shows only the object and its background. (See page 27 for how to take a vertical photo.)

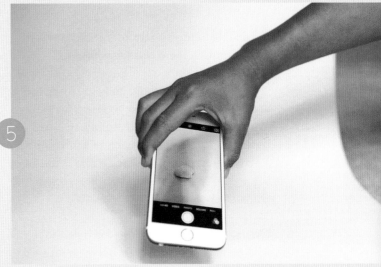

6. Repeat steps 4 and 5 for each object, using a different color each time or alternating between a couple of different colors.

7. Print the photos on photo paper so they are all the same size. 4 x 6 inches (about half a piece of paper) works well.

8. Using the scissors, cut away the white borders so that the photos show only the object and colored backdrop.

TIP A still life is a picture of objects (not people).

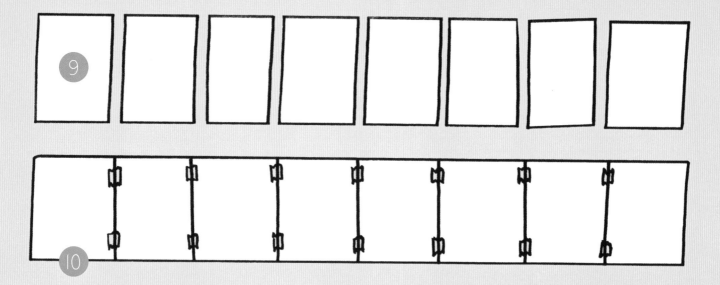

Make the accordion book:

9 On a table, lay the photos out in an order you like, and place them close together.

10 Turn the photos over, and make sure the edges are touching and that they are lined up top-to-bottom. Tape them together along the back edges. Turn them over afterward to make sure everything is right-side-up and in the right place. You should now have all the photos connected, taped together in a row.

11 On small scraps of paper (maybe different colored paper), write a short poem about each object (or you can write a poetic description). "A very sharp shark's tooth"; "winners in the epic mini-golf battle"; "rainy day friendship bracelets"; and so on.

12 Using just a thin layer of glue, attach the poems/descriptions to the back of each photograph. The back of the photos with the poems/descriptions will be the inside of your book (once it's finished).

13 Fold up the pages along the places where you taped each page. You are folding the pages like an accordion so they come together as a single book.

TIP Instead of an accordion book, you can also make a poster using the pictures of your favorite objects.

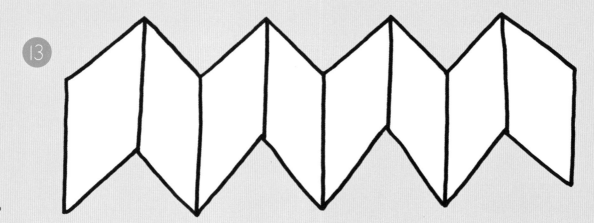

Make the book cover:

14 Cut a piece of poster board to about the same size as the pictures to make the front cover. Make another one the same size for the back cover.

15 Write the book's title on the front cover (The Beach!), and decorate the front and back covers using the art supplies, if you wish.

16 Tape the front cover to the edge of the first picture (the same way you taped the pictures together). Repeat for the back cover/last page. To hide the tape from showing on the cover, try gluing a strip of paper down the edge of the book over the exposed tape.

17 When you open the book, you'll see the photographs that describe the place. When you flip it over, the picture captions make a poem about it.

TIP You can flip through the still life accordion as a book, or open it fully to display the whole thing and set it out on your dresser, shelf, or mantle.

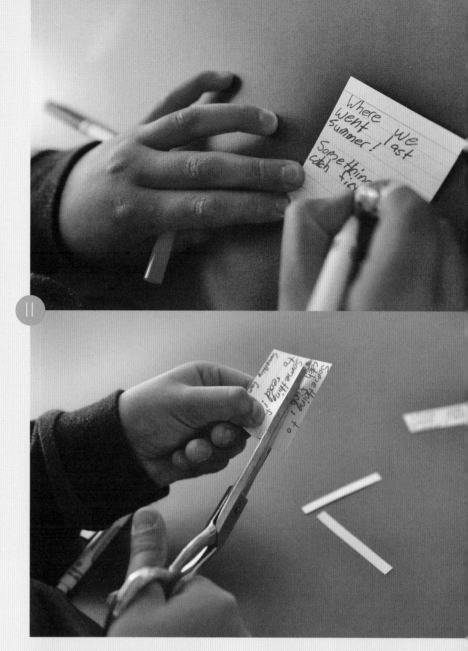

Neighbor- hood Map

The Prickily Berry Bush

WHOF!

ouch!

The Park

a awesomazing time!

BFF's

Neighbor- Hood Map

Explore your neighborhood with a camera and photograph all of the landmarks that are important to you and make your own personalized map. If you ever get lost near your house or have an unfortunate accident with a memory-erasing machine in the garage, this map will get you home and remind you of all of your favorite things.

stuff you'll need:

- [ ] Camera
- [ ] Computer and printer
- [ ] Photo paper
- [ ] Scissors
- [ ] Big piece of paper (about 3 feet wide) or a bunch of sheets taped together to make a big piece
- [ ] Extra paper (any size is fine)
- [ ] Markers, paint, and art supplies
- [ ] Tape or glue
- [ ] **2 to 3 hours**

let's do this!

1 Go for a walk around your neighborhood with your camera. Pick a familiar route, like the way to the park, a friend's house, or your school.

2 Keep an eye out for the places and sights that you see every time you walk on this route, and pay attention to the memories that pop up while you're walking. Maybe you see your best friend's house or the sledding hill where you made the ramp last year, the tree you used to like to climb, the place where you buried your hamster when he died, or the creek where you sometimes go fishing.

3 When you see a familiar or favorite place, stop and take a photograph of it.

Try to make a picture that shows how you feel. Use a worm's-eye view (from the ground or below your subject) to make your subject look big and frightening, important, or brave. Or use a bird's-eye view (from above) to make things look tiny and insignificant. You can also use light to show your feelings and opinions: your favorite tree could be flooded with warm evening light; maybe you photograph an old, sad house with a shadow across it.

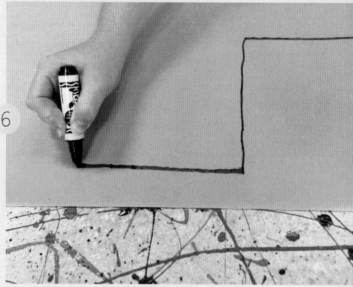

4 Take at least 10 photographs. Print out small versions of them on photo paper (you can use the scale function to shrink them when you go to print them or print multiple pictures on a page). Cut out the small photos.

5 To make the map, arrange the photos on the big piece of paper in the order you walked by them. Don't glue the photos to the paper yet (this comes later!), and be sure to leave extra space between the photos so that you can draw roads and paths between them. Tape more pieces of paper to your big piece of paper, if you need more room for your photos.

6 Use markers or paint to draw the roads and sidewalks that connect the places you photographed.

7 Glue the photographs to the map.

TIPS

Your neighborhood map doesn't have to be perfectly to scale. Just as long as you recognize your route, the distances can be a little wonky.

After making the map of all of your favorite places, try walking around the neighborhood and taking pictures of things you normally just walk by without really looking at (like the store window that never changes, the bus stop, the path leading into the woods). Sometimes, the everyday things you walk by are the most interesting to the camera! Add these pictures to the map you've already made, or make a new, everyday map.

You could also make a nature map that shows your favorite plants, trees, or rock formations; or a friend map that shows where your buddies live; or a map of the fastest hills for biking, the best hiding places, or any theme you're an expert on.

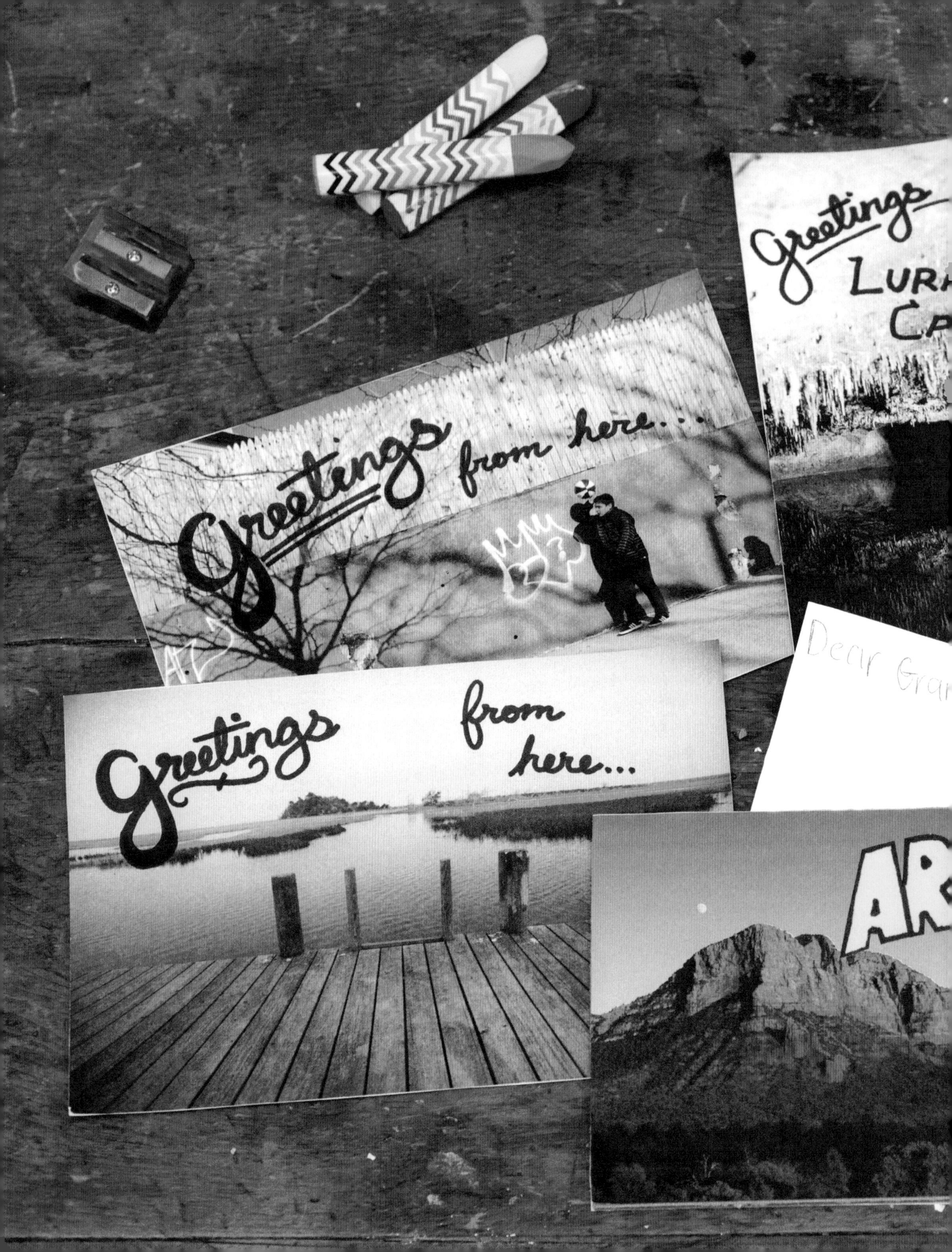
Greetings from here...
Greetings from here...
Greetings

greetings FROM HERE

greetings from here

You've probably seen the sights in your hometown a million times, and by now they're not that amazing to you anymore. But what if you were seeing them for the first time again? Pretend you're visiting your hometown as a tourist to see the most interesting places near your home afresh. Take glorious, postcard-like photographs of them that you can mail to friends and family or keep for yourself.

stuff you'll need:

- [ ] Camera
- [ ] Adult helper
- [ ] Computer and printer
- [ ] Photo paper
- [ ] Poster board
- [ ] Glue stick
- [ ] Scissors
- [ ] Pen
- [ ] Postcard stamps (optional)
- [ ] **An afternoon**

TIPS

To take the most glorious pictures, you need to photograph at the right time of day. Go out in the early morning or in the late afternoon, when the light makes the place look beautiful and special. And, pick the best point of view, where everything looks clean and lovely and you can't see the parking lot or the garbage cans.

When you take your photos, pay attention to composition. "Composition" is the way that the shapes are arranged inside the frame: Is the round moon right above the pointy mountain? Is the line of cars making a curly line at the bottom of the photograph? Lines are almost always interesting. Try to include a few lines (like the horizon, sidewalks, or fences) in your photo.

You could also do a sarcastic version of "Greetings from Here," by taking a beautifully lit photograph of a garbage dump or a traffic jam.

let's do this!

1 On a piece of paper, make a list of the sights in your city or town. Where do you always go on class trips? Which part of your city is full of tourists? What is your town known for? World's largest apples? Some kind of fancy bridge? A canyon that's very grand? If your town isn't known for anything in particular, what kinds of things do you think are interesting about it? Is there a railroad? Is there a park? An old tree with beautiful leaves? Put these things on your list.

2 Ask your helper to take you to your favorite tourist attraction(s) or interesting places so you can take photographs to make into a series of postcards. Use beautiful light, thoughtful composition, and careful framing to really make the place look great. For suggestions on working with light, read the "Go to the Light" section (see page 8) in the Fun Rules.

3 Print the photographs 4 x 6 inches large onto photo paper (this size is important if you plan on mailing them, because anything larger requires more stamps). If a photo prints out in a different size, you can always have white space around it or crop it to be 4 x 6 inches.

4 Glue the back of the photographs to the poster board so they are less floppy, and then cut them out. (Remember to keep them 4 x 6 inches.)

5 Write a note on the back of a postcard, and drop it in the mail, if you want to mail it. (Remember to leave room for the address and stamp!) You could even mail a postcard to yourself. Or, you can just keep the postcards and display them in your home. Or, you could make a postcard album: see how to make a blank book (pages 60-61).

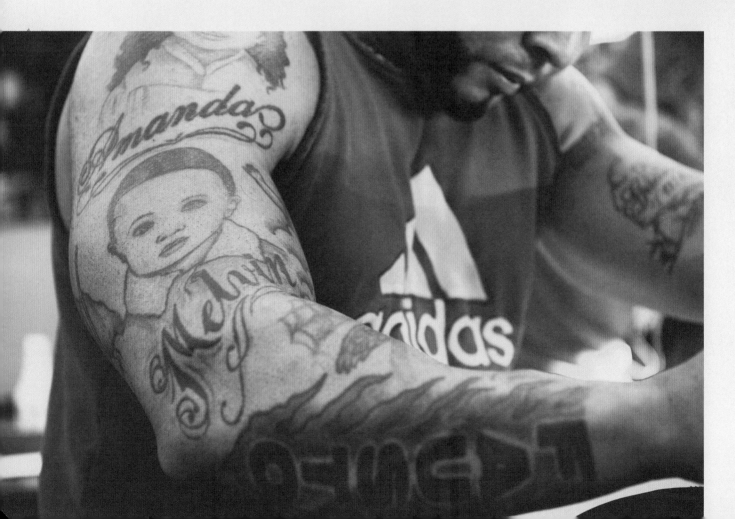

a Day iN THE LiFE

a Day iN THE LiFE

How can you tell a person's true story with photographs? Here, you will think like a reporter and interview an older person you care about to find out what he or she really does all day. You will go with the person to his or her workplace, and take photographs while you're there. Later, you will create a photo story about a day in his or her life.

stuff you'll need:

- [ ] Camera
- [ ] Adult
- [ ] Paper and pen
- [ ] Computer and printer
- [ ] Photo paper
- [ ] **Half a day**

5

let's do this!

1. Sit down with an adult you like talking to. It could be your grandmother, a parent, a family friend. Just make sure it's someone who does work you're curious about. It would be lots of fun to photograph someone whose job is interesting to look at, like a barber or zookeeper. But, even someone who works in an office could be a great subject to interview, and you could find interesting things to photograph there, too.

2. Ask the adult about their daily schedule. When do interesting things happen? When could you go take pictures of him or her?

3. Go to your subject's job for a few hours. While you're there, take photographs that tell the story of the person's work, like these:

   — Action shots.
   — A wide shot that shows your subject in their workplace (the whole barber shop with the subject working at a chair).
   — A close-up of your subject's hands doing their work (hands using the scissors to cut hair).
   — Details that tell us about the place and the work (a table with brushes, clippers, and spray bottle).
   — A portrait of the person at work (you can tell them how to pose, or just take a photograph of their face).

4. At home, print out your photos on photo paper, and choose the 5 best. 4 x 6 inch prints work well.

5. Later, show your best 5 photographs to your subject. Ask him or her to write a caption for each photograph: a sentence explaining what's happening in each picture and what the person is working on at the job. Or, you write the captions based on what you know from the visit.

6. Make the photographs and captions into a little book for your subject (see pages 60–61 for easy instructions on how to make a blank book).

TIPS

A subject is the person in a photograph.

A wide shot shows most everything in the scene.

A close-up shows a small part of the scene.

If you start to feel uncomfortable or shy, take a picture. There, no longer awkward! Oh, still feeling a little weird? Take another one! Now make a joke, stretch a little, drink some water, and pretend you feel like the most confident photographer in the known universe. A lot of a photographer's job is waiting for something to happen and trying to find interesting photographs when you don't think there are any left. Don't stop taking photographs the first time you want to. Stick it out, you can do it!

DAY!!!

TiME
CAPSULE

TiME CAPSULE

A visual gift to your future self, featuring photos of things and people important to you.

stuff you'll need:

- [ ] Camera
- [ ] Friends and family
- [ ] Computer and printer
- [ ] Photo paper
- [ ] Pen and paper
- [ ] Small box
- [ ] Packing tape
- [ ] Markers, construction paper, and art supplies
- [ ] **1 hour to an afternoon, depending**

SHOES

PHOTO
PAPER

pen

New favorite joke: A giraffe falls asleep on the ground. A rhino asks a bird, "What's that lyin' there?" The bird answers, "That's not a lion, that's a giraffe!"

DON'T OPEN UNTIL 11ᵀᴴ B-DAY!!!

let's do this!

1   On a piece of paper, make a list of objects that are important to you. Things like your skateboard, favorite shoes, necklace your grandmother gave you, dirt bike, softest pillow, etc.

2   Gather the objects together, and photograph them against a neutral background: lean them against a blank wall, or place each item on a tabletop or floor and take the picture from above. Make sure you have enough light to take a clear picture of each object.

3   Make a list of the places that matter to you, and photograph as many of them as you can.

4   Make a list of your best friends, and shoot a portrait of each of them.

5   Take a selfie in your favorite t-shirt or outfit.

6   Look at all your pictures, choose the best photographs, and print them out on photo paper.

7   Also, on a piece of paper, write down a favorite joke, a prediction about next year, and a goal or reminder about something that matters to you right now, at this moment in time. You could also draw a picture, write a poem, or write a letter to your future self.

8   Put the photographs and notes into a small box and tape it closed. Decorate it if you like. Write the date your time capsule will be opened on top of the box. The date should be 1 year from the date you are closing up the box. Store your time capsule somewhere safe. Put a reminder to yourself on the calendar so you don't forget!

9   Wait 365 days.

10   Open the box!

TIP   You could do this on your birthday, before the last day of school, or on another important day.

For Nick, William, and January:
my home.

Thank you to the children who
collaborated with me to make these
pictures: Prayer and Noble
Young-Blackgoat; Ariel Burgos,
Crystal Carrion, Melvin Recio,
Romeo Rios, Cristian Vasquez, and
Luis Yaport; and Abigael Ellerglick
and Harper Tidwell.

Thank you also to Denise Wolff for
her ideas and direction; to David
Arkin for his skill with robots and
paper craft; to Gordon Baldwin of
M.S. 136 in Brooklyn, Fausto Recio of
Fausto Stilo Barbershop, Heidi and
Cullen Young-Blackgoat, Lisa Eller,
Jennifer Hoyt Tidwell, and Courtney
and Alex Epton for letting me
photograph in their classroom,
barbershop, and homes; to Emily
Lessard for this exciting book
design and to Maggie Prendergast
for her lovely illustrations; to
Nicole Moulaison for her work on
the production of the book; to
Susan Ciccotti, Amelia Lang, and
Jonathan Knight Newhall for their
help behind the scenes at Aperture;
to Sarah McNear for her support;
and to Paula Szuchman and to
Amy Alvarez for endless, invaluable
honesty and encouragement.

—Alice Proujansky

Go Photo!
An Activity Book for Kids
Texts and photographs by Alice Proujansky
Illustrations by Maggie Prendergast

Editor: Denise Wolff
Designer: Emily Lessard
Production Director: Nicole Moulaison
Production Manager: Thomas Bollier
Craft Master: David Arkin
Assistant Editor: Jonathan Knight Newhall
Copy Editor: Catherine Field
Senior Text Editor: Susan Ciccotti
Proofreader: Madeline Coleman
Work Scholars: Cassidy Paul and Sophie Klafter

Collaborators and Models: Abigael Ellerglick
and Harper Tidwell of Charlottesville, Virginia;
Prayer and Noble Young-Blackgoat, and their
parents Cullen and Heidi Young-Blackgoat of
Flagstaff; Ariel Burgos, Crystal Carrion, Romeo
Rios, Cristian Vasquez, and Luis Yaport of
Middle School 136 in Brooklyn; Ben and Sara
Wolff of Fort Mill, South Carolina; and Melvin,
Amanda, Yadiel, and Fausto Recio of the
Fausto Stilo Barbershop in Brooklyn

Additional staff of the Aperture book
program includes:
Chris Boot, Executive Director; Sarah McNear,
Deputy Director; Lesley A. Martin, Creative
Director; Kellie McLaughlin, Director of
Sales and Marketing; Amelia Lang, Managing
Editor; Samantha Marlow, Assistant Editor;
Katie Clifford, Executive Assistant and
Project Editor; Taia Kwinter, Assistant to the
Managing Editor

Typeset in Avenir Next, created by Adrian
Frutiger and Akira Kobayashi, and Honeybun,
created by Emily Lessard

First edition
Printed in China
10 9 8 7 6 5 4 3 2 1

Library of Congress Control Number:
2015959630
ISBN 978-1-59711-355-7

To order Aperture books, contact:
212-946-7154
orders@aperture.org

For information about Aperture trade
distribution worldwide, visit:
www.aperture.org/distribution

aperture

Aperture Foundation
547 West 27th Street, 4th Floor
New York, N.Y. 10001
www.aperture.org

Aperture, a not-for-profit foundation,
connects the photo community and its
audiences with the most inspiring work,
the sharpest ideas, and with each other—
in print, in person, and online.